John Joseph Lynch

Pastoral letter of the Right Rev. John Joseph Lynch, Bishop

of Toronto

to the Clergy and Laity of the Diocese Promulgating the Jubilee

John Joseph Lynch

Pastoral letter of the Right Rev. John Joseph Lynch, Bishop of Toronto
to the Clergy and Laity of the Diocese Promulgating the Jubilee

ISBN/EAN: 9783337064884

Printed in Europe, USA, Canada, Australia, Japan

Cover: Foto ©Lupo / pixelio.de

More available books at **www.hansebooks.com**

PASTORAL LETTER

OF THE

RIGHT REV. JOHN JOSEPH LYNCH,

BISHOP OF TORONTO,

TO THE

CLERGY AND LAITY OF THE DIOCESE,

PROMULGATING THE JUBILEE.

TOGETHER WITH THE

LATE ENCYCLICAL OF THE HOLY FATHER,

AND THE

SYLLABUS OF ERRORS CONDEMNED.

TORONTO:

PRINTED AND PUBLISHED BY J. G. MOYLAN, OFFICE OF THE
"CANADIAN FREEMAN," No. 74 CHURCH STREET.

1865.

PASTORAL LETTER

OF

HIS LORDSHIP THE BISHOP OF TORONTO.

JOHN JOSEPH LYNCH,

By the Grace of God *and the authority of the Holy and Apostolic See, Bishop of Toronto, Assistant at the Pontifical Throne, &c., to the Venerable Clergy and beloved Faithful of our Diocese, salvation and benediction from our Lord.*

Our Holy Father Pope Pius IX., successor of St. Peter, the Prince of the Apostles, in the plenitude of powers conceded to him by our Lord and Saviour Jesus Christ, typified by the keys of the Kingdom of Heaven (Matt. xvi. 18, 19), opens for the fifth time during his eventful pontificate of eighteen years, those celestial gates of mercy and grace in favour of the redeemed of Christ. It is our pleasing duty, as well as our privilege to be the willing medium of communicating to you, Beloved Brethren, the happy intelligence, that our Holy Father grants a plenary indulgence in form of Jubilee to all the faithful, who being heartily penitent, shall have confessed their sins, and being absolved by an approved priest, and having received Holy Communion, given alms, visited the Churches and fasted, will pray for the graces desired by the Sovereign Pontiff.

The reasons for granting a Jubilee at this especial time are twofold: First, that the faithful being purified in the probatic well of penance, and strengthened with the celestial banquet of our Lord's Body, by fasting, alms and prayer, might obtain from our merciful Lord the conversion of sinners and peace for the Church; "that Pagans quitting their idols may acknowledge one God and Jesus Christ His Son the Redeemer of the world;" "that heretics and schismatics acknowledging their errors may return to the unity of the truth," being of one mind and one spirit, form one body and one fold under the one Shepherd in the Church established by our Lord Jesus Christ; that all governors may rule for the happiness, and not for the destruction of their subjects; that famine and pestilence, the scourge of God for sins, may be averted; that war, the scourge of man, with all its dread and horrid consequences, may be kept far from us; that, in fine, the entire human family would turn to God their Sovereign Lord and last end, and worship Him with sincerity and truth, and seek with all their hearts above all things, the Kingdom of God (Math. vi. 33).

The second motive for granting the Jubilee seems to be, to gather closer into the bosom of the Church, the fold of Christ, by the means of the sacraments, all of the household of the faith, that they, being separated from false brethren, may be instructed and strengthened against the mighty torrent of error which inundates and carries off into the abyss of destruction the proud, the covetous, the luxurious, the negligent, and those who despise the teachings of Christ through His Church.

Our Holy Father the Pope, as chief watchman and pilot at the helm of the bark of Peter, which is freighted with pearls of great price—immortal souls,—" bought with the blood of Jesus Christ" (1 Corinth., chap. vi.), points out to his children the rocks of error which they are to avoid, if they wish to arrive at the harbor of rest in the bosom of God. Accompanying his gracious decree of an universal Jubilee, he has sent to the Bishops of the Church an Encyclical Letter, with a Syllabus of condemned propositions embodying the errors of modern times pernicious in their tendency, and fruitful in evil.

Already, beloved brethren, you have been made acquainted with the Encyclical and the Syllabus. We endeavored, in a few lectures, delivered in our Cathedral in Toronto, to explain those propositions comprised in the Syllabus which appear to be most misunderstood and maliciously interpreted. We also, on Passion Sunday, 2nd of April, caused the Encyclical and Syllabus to be read by our Secretary in the vernacular language at High Mass; and, then, in the said Cathedral, we solemnly in our name, and in the name of our clergy and people, received the Papal Decrees, condemned in the sense of our Holy Father all errors condemned by him, and holding all doctrines proclaimed by him *ex cathedra*, knowing that in adhering to the Pope we adhere to Peter, and in adhering to Peter we adhere to Christ. The words of our Divine Redeemer, " He that hears you hears me" (Luke x. 16), may be emphatically applied to the Sovereign Pontiff.

The Encyclical and Syllabus of condemned propositions aroused a furious storm in the world. The nations roared with fury, and meditated and said foolish things. The proud kings of the earth stood amazed at being rebuked for their bad faith, their lying policy, and oppression of the weak. Their ministers and scribes tried to write down with ridicule and misrepresentation, and cover up in abuse the authority that condemned the errors and vices, and opposed the passions and prejudices of the age. The angry billows of yesterday are the tiny waves of to-day. The storm of impotent rage has calmed down, and we can now serenely look over the subsiding billows. Do any fragments of the wreck or spars from the bark of Peter strew the sea? Oh no! the goodly ship has breasted the rage of the storm: Jesus is in the ship: Behold I am with you all days even to the consummation of the world (Matt. xxvi. 20). Jesus awakened rebukes the wind, and the raging of the waters, and the storm ceased and there was a calm (Luke viii. 24).

The howling of the storm proved, first, that the world was surrounded with a pestiferous atmosphere; that the equilibrium of its social and religious elements was disturbed, right was called wrong and wrong right. Secondly, that there is a public conscience; for it must exist, to show signs of life. It was disturbed, it was annoyed, it chafed under rebuke, or, as a sick child, fretted and stormed against the kind physician that tried to apply remedies for its cure. Thousands outside the Church rejoiced that a hero was found in the venerable person of the Head of the Catholic Church, who had the courage to raise his voice to condemn the fatal errors and delusive prejudices of the age.

Thirdly, the fury of the storm proved that he who condemned errors had the authority from on high to do so, otherwise his condemnation would not be heeded. If the head of any of the so-called churches, whether they be crowned heads, or the elected of their own body, issue a mandate condemning errors, would their voice be heard beyond their own society? Nay, would not their authority for condemning errors be denied, since the right of private judgment, which permits every man to hold or reject whatsoever truth or error he pleases, was made one of the fundamental principles of *their* religion so-called? The Bishop of Rome speaks, and two hundred millions of Catholics, spread over the entire world, with their Bishops and Priests, listen with attention, and receive with reverential submission the teachings of their Chief Pastor, who holds the place of Christ on earth. As the words of Christ were misinterpreted, so were the words of his Vicar on earth; as Christ was reviled, so was the Pope. The disciple is not above the master (Matt. x. 24).

The Sovereign Pontiff condemns errors that should be condemned by every man of sense and by every christian of sound principles. We shall give a synopsis of the condemned propositions.

1.—Pantheism, Naturalism and Rationalism.

What sane man will not condemn, with the Pope, the error that affirms that God is nature, stones, trees, reptiles, air, water, &c.; that God is consequently mutable, composed of every thing? The insane alone could have imagined such a theory as this. And again, that God has nothing to do with the laws that govern the material world, and has no action over the destinies of man? That human reason is the source of the truths of religion; as if human reason could have invented the idea of the Trinity, the divine Incarnation, the parturition of a virgin. What absurdities in those two propositions! Divine revelation is imperfect; Christian faith is in opposition to human reason. Christian faith is of the supernatural order, and consequently above human reason, not in opposition to it. Nothing so conformable to human reason than to submit to an infallible authority revealing mysteries. "Faith," says St. Paul, "is the substance of things hoped for, the conviction of things that appear not" (Heb. xi). What christian will say, with Colenzo, that the predictions of the prophets of the old law are fables; or, with Strauss, that Christ is a myth? And still those men were not authoritatively silenced by their sects.

How detestable the pride of those who say that this weak fallen human reason of ours is on a level with religion! So, theological matters or divine truths are to be treated philosophically, that is, submitted to the test of reason, to be admitted or rejected by it; thus setting up human reason as judge, and consequently superior to the divine reason or light of God.

2.—Indifferentism, Latitudinarianism.

True religion when embraced and practised guarantees to man the possession of eternal life; religion therefore should not be a subject of indifference. If a person wishes to invest money in a property that he hopes to enjoy for many years, does he not take pains, does he not seek learned advice, does he, without examining title deeds, plunge into the depths of a contract from which he will not be easily liberated. Our Lord has said, "The children of this generation are wiser than the children of light." Christ has warned his disciples against false teachers (Math. vii. 15). And St. Peter, 2nd Ep. ii. 2, "But as there were false prophets among the people even so there shall be lying teachers amongst you who will bring in sects of perdition. In the last time there shall come mockers walking in their own desires in impurity." Will any one say that there are no false religions and doctrines in the world? Will any one say that all the so-called religions differing amongst themselves are the inspirations of the spirit of God? The fact of the existence of so many Churches proves that they hold opposing doctrines, otherwise sects would have no occasion to split and divide, and reorganise and build different places of worship.

Is a man to be less prudent in embracing and practising the true religion on which his eternal happiness depends, than men of the world in seeking worldly gain?

Could the Spirit of God dictate contrary and contradictory creeds? No wonder then that our holy Father should condemn the error that affirms, no matter what religion man embraces, he may be saved in it, whether Buddhism, Mormonism, or any other absurdism of the age. He repudiates the idea that a man is free to embrace and profess the religion which he considers true, guided by the light of reason alone. God must be the guide to the true religion, and His divine grace must attract the mind and heart to it. No one can come to the Son except the Father attract him (St. John vi. 44). The religion in which is found salvation must be the religion established by our Lord Jesus Christ. There is no other name whereby man may be saved (Acts iv. 12).

The condemnation of the 18th Proposition of the Syllabus, sounds disagreeably in Protestant ears. "Protestantism is nothing more than another form of the same true religion, in which it is possible to be equally pleasing to God as in the Catholic Church."

Protestantism is hard to define. It is a negation, and excludes properties; but to appropriate a meaning to it, let us call it the sum of all the various creeds composed by the different founders of those innumerable sects which have sprung up at and since the Reformation.

We have then the collection of the various opinions, interpretations of texts of the Bible, peculiar views, strange systems of faith, all protesting their falibility; in fine, a babel of confusion, all jarring amongst themselves, but agreeing to oppose the Catholic Church and misrepresent her doctrines. Do the various Protestant creeds concede to each other the possibility of attaining salvation in their peculiar tenets? Do the Anglicans consider that the Unitarians, who deny the divinity of Christ, will be saved? Do the Baptists, who believe that immersion is a necessary condition of membership in the church of Christ, admit that the unbaptised and unimmersed will be saved, when they quote the words of our Lord, except a person be regenerated in water and the Holy Spirit he cannot enter the kingdom of God? (John iii. 5.) We might quote extensively from the several confessions of faith of various sects that are exclusive in their claims of salvation for themselves alone, but the bounds of a pastoral will not admit of this. At any rate they hold that the benighted Catholics believe idolatrous doctrines, and to be crowned some sovereigns had to swear to this. Will idolaters be saved? Catholics are by many Protestants excluded from the kingdom of heaven. Has man received from Christ the privilege of framing his own creed, and to believe as much or as little as he pleases, to perform as much or as little as he may opine? No. Man must believe all the truths revealed by Christ, " and to enter into life he must keep the commandments." The road that leadeth to eternal life was traced out by our Lord and Saviour Jesus Christ. It is difficult and narrow, and few find it, or desire to walk in it. It costs much self-denial to submit the reason and will to the obedience of faith, and the human passions to the yoke of the gospel. Do we find men at the period of the so-called reformation seeking the difficult path of penance, mortification, fasting, confession of sins, voluntary poverty, chastity, obedience to the divinely appointed authority left by Christ in his Church? We find quite the contrary. And are we to admit that, no matter what a man believes, he will be saved; and that those that practice none of the rules of christianity, and reject the sacraments instituted by Jesus Christ for the salvation of souls, will be saved equally with those who do practice all? We might as well say that those that sow nothing will reap abundantly, as to affirm this. It is therefore absurd to say that the complete code of doctrine revealed by Christ can be found in the various warring creeds that constitute Protestantism; and that it can be as pleasing to God to believe in these mutilated systems of Christianity, as to embrace all the truth that is in " Christ Jesus," and to belong to the one fold under the one " shepherd."

From this we are not to conclude that all those who die apparently in Protestantism are lost. We admit an invincible ignorance, that is, that some are so debarred by the circumstances of their position, education and early prejudices, instilled into their tender minds by parents and teachers that they were bound to respect, as to be placed in a moral " impossibility" of knowing the truth, and who are otherwise of pure morals and follow the natural law and its precepts, engraven by God on the hearts of all, and are quite prepared to embrace the truth at any sacrifice when sufficiently known; these, we say, belong to the soul of the Church, and are in the way of salvation. On this point we delight to quote the very words of our Holy Father:

" It is known indeed to us and to you, that those who labor under invincible ignorance concerning our most holy religion, and who lead a virtuous and correct life, sedulously keeping the natural law and its precepts engraven by God on the hearts of all, and prepared to obey

God, (that these men) are able through the operation of divine light and grace to obtain eternal life ; since God, who clearly sees, searches and knows the minds, dispositions, thoughts and habits of all men, according to his supreme goodness and mercy, does not permit that any one should suffer eternal punishment who has not on him the guilt of voluntary fault." But the number of those is known only to God. We fear, alas, it is but too small. Worldliness, pride and indifference in religious matters leave many on the broad road that leadeth to eternal destruction. Neither the bad Catholic who does not practice his religion, nor the Protestant, careless of seeking the truth or praying to attain it, can reasonably expect the "kingdom which suffereth violence, and which the violent alone bear away."

Errors against the Church and its Rights.

The Church founded by our blessed Lord for the conversion of the whole world was endowed with the necessary powers of existence, conservation and action. It is a perfectly independent spiritual kingdom, with means and help to work out the intentions of its Divine Founder; it should not therefore be entrammelled in its action by the world which it was established to convert and subject to the yoke of Christ. This is clear from the commission given the Church by our Lord Jesus Christ in the words that follow : "All power is given to me in heaven and on earth. Going, therefore, teach ye all nations," Math. xviii. 19. This broad commission, wide as the world and universal as mankind, implied on the part of the nations a correlative duty of listening to the teachings of the Church and of obeying its laws. And this is the sense in which the commission was understood by the Apostles themselves, for we read in the Acts of the Apostles (c. iv. 19), that when St. Peter and St. John were charged by the council not to speak at all nor teach in the name of Jesus, they answered and said, "If it be just in the sight of God to hear ye rather than God, judge ye" "We ought to obey God rather than man" (Acts v. 19).

Councils were held by the Church of God, and the Apostles asked not the permission of the secular power to do so. They framed decrees and solicited not the royal or imperial *exequatur* for their promulgation. St. Paul excommunicated the incestuous Corinthian without asking the permission of the civil authority of his time. And yet we do not find that any royal decree was published (as would undoubtedly occur under similar circumstances in the regenerated States of to-day) to punish Paul with exile or imprisonment, for daring to exercise this striking act of spiritual jurisdiction without the authorization of Cæsar. In fact, history is there to prove that the Church never recognized in the civil power of the State the right to trammel its independence, or to control its purely spiritual acts. The Apostles, as we have seen, utterly repudiated the notion of such a right. The Church of the first three centuries asserted its independence of the civil power in the gloom of the catacombs, as well as on the red scaffold of martyrdom. Descending from that date, we shall find that the Church in the many vicissitudes of its history has always vindicated its right to the liberty of prosecuting its heavenly mission independently of state control or bureauemtic despotism. The doctrine of the encyclical on this point is therefore no new doctrine—it is as old as the Church—it is the doctrine always taught in the Church, and which it will continue to teach unto the end.

If the spirit of the world is to be found on earth, it truly must be found in the courts of kings. Would even human prudence have suggested that kings and rulers of this earth should have the control of the gospel of penance, humility, mortification and self-denial? No! It is repugnant to the spirit of the gospel that the preachers of the Word of God, and ministers of His sacred mysteries, should be the tools and serfs of kings or rulers of this world, and that the power of the Word should be under their control; or their temporalities, subject to be sequestered at the beck of a worldling, reproved for his vices. Herod, though very wicked, respected and feared St. John Baptist, but like others heated with wine, consented to the perpetration of murder to please an adulteress and her deluded daughter (St. Mark vi. 27). Thus have the bishops and priests of the Church been sacrificed to the despotic rule of corrupt legislators and their unholy favorites and minions. (See *Life of St. John Chrysothom, St. Basil,* and others).

The Catholic Church is not alone in its repudiation of the unholy claims of the State to control religion. Nonconformists, Independents, Presbyterians, Methodists, Baptists, in fact the whole body of Dissenters, and at present a vast number in the Church of England, ignore the idea that spiritual supremacy is centred in the head of the State. Henry VIII. of England, we believe, was the first among Christian princes that imitated the pagan emperors, to arrogate to himself spiritual supremacy. And oh! what a monster to receive such homage. The gospel of Christ was delivered to be preached to emperors and princes, and God demands that they be as submissive to its divine law as the lowliest of their subjects.

Errors concerning the Education of Youth.

The Church of God has always claimed the chief control in the education of her children. The Church of God received the commission to teach all nations. Children as well as parents are included in the injunction given in this commission. The Church says with Christ, "Suffer little children to come unto me and forbid them not, for of such is the kingdom of heaven." The Church receives the child from the knee of its parent into her schools, and imbues its tender mind with the fear of God, gives it a knowledge of His holy law, and prepares it to take its stand in society by imparting to it secular knowledge. And in doing this the Church does not usurp or infringe upon parental rights. On the contrary, she supplies what parents, immersed in the concerns of life, have no time or education sufficient themselves to furnish. Hence the prelates of the Catholic Church, even during periods of great poverty, and when trammelled by impediments from the State, struggles equally for the propagation of the gospel, and for the Catholic education of youth. "The same roof," says the canon of St. Patrick, "should cover the Church and the school." The Bishops of England at present have wisely decreed to have school-chapels, that is, buildings to be used as schools during the week, and as chapels on Sundays, in localities too poor to have distinct edifices for both purposes. A celebrated French publicist has well said, "I will guarantee to have the nation of any faith, or of no faith, as you please, if you place in my hands the education of the people for twenty years." Teach a child Paganism, and he will be Pagan; Christianity and he will be Christian. How sad, yet how true it is that leading revolutionary statesmen imbued with infidel and irreligious ideas labor to have the minds of the rising generation so fashioned, as to make them their willing tools and blind instruments, and strange to say, these very men are sedulously careful to have their own children, and especially their daughters, educated in the strict principles of Christianity.

We therefore, beloved Brethren, following in the footsteps of our saintly predecessors, and in conformity with the spirit of the Church, exhort all parents to endeavor to fulfil their duty by procuring a Catholic education for their children: "Train up a child in the way he shall go, and when he grows old he shall not depart from it;" for, as St. Paul says, "he that neglecteth his household is worse than an infidel."

Errors concerning Natural and Christian Ethics.

Our Holy Father condemns the foolish error of those who say that moral laws do not stand in need of the divine sanction; that right consists in the material fact; that authority is nothing else than the result of universal superiority and material force; that the sanctity of right is acquired by brute force, as though a robber has a right to your purse, if he have strength and force enough to keep it; just as the five kings of Sodom would have acquired a right to the booty which they carried off, if Abraham had not force enough to re-conquer them; or as Victor Emmanuel has a right to those kingdoms which he usurped, merely because his neighbours are too weak to oppose him. Would the Queen of England willingly cede her rights to her possessions to a more powerful nation able to wrest them from her? By no means; there are certain rights and trusts which can neither be justly invaded, nor rightfully surrendered.

The principle of *non-intervention*, as it is called, is a convenient doctrine invented by usurpers, who used the *intervention* of powerful allies to add to their dominions, and now, when tolerably secure in .their usurpation, they proclaim non-intervention to prevent weak and dethroned monarchs from obtaining assistance to re-conquer their plundered possessions. Europe did not hold this doctrine of non-intervention when it combined against Napoleon I. or the present Emperor of France in the affairs of Italy.

Rich individuals are bound to succour their neighbours in distress. Powerful monarchs are bound to protect their weaker fellow-princes to maintain, for the public good, their just rights, when it can be done without great inconvenience. Such is the law of charity in individuals and nations.

Our Holy Father displeases the revolutionists by condemning the proposition which asserts that "it is allowable to refuse obedience to legitimate princes; nay more, to rise in insurrection against them." This is a general proposition and admits of an exception. The proposition does not say that it is *never* permitted to disobey princes. They must be disobeyed when they order anything at variance with the law of God, as a child is bound to disobey his parents under similar circumstances. The second part of the proposition does not say either that revolt against princes is *never* permissible. A legitimate prince may forfeit his legitimacy by violating the contract expressed or implied upon his assuming the reins of government, when he governs for the destruction and not for the edification and happiness of his people. In these cases to disobey princes, or even to revolt against them, is not condemned by the Church.

The Roman Pontiffs always opposed tyrants and succoured the oppressed. In the dark night of feudal oppression and serfdom of the people, the Popes afforded the only refuge against tyrants in the middle ages, when society, under the direction of the Church, was taking form and shape, emerging from the chaos caused by the breaking up of the Roman Empire. Tyrants accuse the Church of favoring revolutionists, and revolutionists, on the other hand, accuse her of protecting tyrants. The Church steers a middle course, she does neither. She rebukes and endeavours to convert tyrants, and she preaches obedience and patience to peoples. Oftentimes her exhortations are unheeded. There is a boundary where she leaves rulers and peoples to seek their rights as best they can, and prays, like Moses on the mountain, that right may prevail over wrong, justice over injustice, liberty over tyranny. She is appalled at uprisings and revolutions, and endeavours to ward them off as long as possible. She dreads the carnage, the sudden death, the cruelty, and the host of crimes worse than death, arising from war. The Church contemplates with dismay the consequences of an unsuccessful revolution — the wholesale confiscations, banishments, executions, and a more intolerable oppression on the part of the victorious, and evils inflicted upon posterity oftentimes worse than those endured by their fathers.

Oh! beloved brethren, when we consider on the one side the sins of the people, and on the other the vices of their rulers—the pride, the thirst for extending dominions by just or unjust means, and the weighing as a drop of water the life's blood of thousands of human beings made to the image and likeness of God, and, as a trifle, the devastation of homes, the scattering of families, and the starvation and dishonour of helpless women and children, we shudder with horror and sicken at the degradation of our poor human nature.

Again, when we read of the lying *fourberie* of governments, politicians and diplomatists, circumventing, watching every opportunity of usurping the possessions of their neighbours, taking advantage of each other in commercial treaties, exchanging all manner of hypocritical courtesies, whilst at the same time they keep immense standing armies as a menace and as a security against the depredations of each other, we are forced to conclude that the good faith and simplicity of the gospel are little heeded by them. One would like to believe in the word of Imperial Majesty; but, alas! now, children only confide in it; and, strange to say, the Bishops of the Church, and even our Holy

Father himself receive lectures and homilies on good government, honesty and ecclesiastical discipline from monarchs and courtiers, whose solemn word and sacred obligations are by them observed only as long as convenient.

Errors concerning Christian Marriage.

Our Holy Father condemns errors respecting Christian marriage. Marriage is the keystone of the social fabric ; disturb it from its position—break its unity—introduce into it dissolvent ingredients, in fine, change it from the condition in which our Lord has placed it, by reversing the decree " What God has joined together let no man separate," and you inundate society with a flood of evils—you open up the flood-gates that stay the tide of human passions, and let that tide loose upon the world. Husbands will become suspicious of their wives, and wives of their husbands. A premium will be offered for infidelity to the marriage obligations ; for the possibility of divorce being once established, and that divorce being obtainable through crime, the espoused would be repudiated for a another of more personal beauty, more fascinating manners, or more ample fortune, and thus the family, which is the very foundation of society, would be dissolved. We have only to refer to the records of the Divorce Court in England to see the workings of this execrable system, which the Holy Father condemns. The *Saturday Review*, a leading Protestant Journal, of January 28, 1865, speaking of this system, says : " The case (a particular case recently decided) has its value, because it seems to have awakened certain suspicions as to the value of that change in the law which has facilitated divorce, the worst fears of those who in the interest of public morality deprecated the change in the marriage laws, have been realized. The plea upon which facilities were given to divorce was of course that of public policy, and in this respect the recent case is an illustrative one (*the present is an odd state of things, which does not conduce the public morality*) ; under the old law it would have been impossible." Thus the Protestants themselves see the evils of their pet system.

Can it be otherwise than degrading, that people should marry for a time, then hold themselves free to separate, and, in the last analysis, what else than this is marriage, when once the law of divorce is admitted ? And how will it fare with the children of divorced parents ? Will they who are commanded to honor, obey and love, their parents, find this commandment easy of observance ? The father is married to

d government,
courtiers, whose
d only as long

OE.

tion marriage.
from its posi-
dients, in fine,
placed it, by
no man sepa-
u open up the
that tide loose
eir wives, and
r infidelity to
o being once
a crime, the
soual beauty,
as the family,
d. We have
nd to see the
er condemns.
January 28,
rticular case
vo awakened
w which has
interest of
, have been
vorce was of
nt case is an
ich does not
have been
rils of their

marry for a
st analysis,
divorce is
d parents?
ir parents,
married to

another woman, and the mother to another man. Alas! for the poor
worse than orphan children!

The Church, holding the place of Christ on earth, is the legitimate guardian of this " great sacrament." She watches over it with a
jealous care; surrounds it with impediments, and by these, as by a
fortress guards its avenues, that none but fit and proper persons may
undertake its obligations. She has always combated the pagan idea
that marriage may be dissolved, but in this she has had no other alternative, since Christ her spouse has uttered the decree, " What God has
joined let no man separate." (Matt. xix. 6).

Errors concerning the Temporal Sovereignty of the Roman Pontiff.

Every true child of the Church recognizes, with the Bishops lately
assembled at Rome, the providential interposition of God in providing
for the Head of the Church an independent Sovereignty. Three hundred years of blood, martyrdom, exile, and persecution of the Church, and
especially of its chief Pastor, the pillage and total ruin of Pagan Rome
by savage conquerors, its abandonment by its emperors and rulers, laid
it prostrate at the feet of the Popes. The people solicited with earnest-
ness to be governed by their kind Apostolic Father and protector, and
the Sovereign Pontiff, not to abandon the tombs of the glorious
Apostles, Peter and Paul, and those arenas drenched by the sacred
blood of tens of thousands of martyrs, acceded to the request of the
people and re-built Rome, preserved and governed it for upwards of
1500 years; and is he now to abandon it to the enemies of Christianity? Three hundred years of persecution prepared the way for this
event, and a multitude of circumstances independent of the will of the
Popes conduced to its accomplishment. Kings respected the Popes for
their wisdom, justice and integrity. People loved the Popes for genuine
philanthropy and paternal care for those who placed themselves under
their protection.

It is true the Popes have been accused by interested parties of
usurpation and even of tyranny in obtaining the provinces which they
now possess; but this is to give the lie to all history. A distinguished
historian, who has deeply studied this question, says: " The establishment of the temporal Sovereignty of the Holy See was not one of
those sudden unforeseen revolutions which astonish the world by the
rapidity of its process. On the contrary, from an attentive perusal of
history, we can trace the steps by which the establishment of that
sovereignty has from a very remote period almost insensibly prepared

and conducted to its issue by a combination of circumstances completely independent of the wills of the Popes—circumstances whose will it was impossible to resist, and whose natural results they could not even counteract without compromising the interests both of religion and society." *Gosselin on the Temporal Power of the Popes.* The temporal power therefore grew up under the protecting shadow of Divine Providence, and is the arrangement of Heaven for the free exercise of the commission conferred by Christ on Peter and his successors. It was fit that the Head of the Christian Church should possess this complete freedom of action, for, if he were a subject, and not a Sovereign he would be entrammelled in the exercise of his jurisdiction, he would be thwarted and obstructed in the government of the universal Church. Abrogate the sovereignty of the Pope, then indeed, in this age of Latitudinarianism, false liberalism and hostility to the true Church, would re-appear the catacombs, and prisons, and exiles. But when those first days of the Church shall have returned, then the last days of the world will be at hand. The states of the Church are a sacred trust confided to the Sovereign Pontiff; they are not his private property; he has them only in trust for the entire Church, and he cannot therefore dispose of them. We ourselves have a Cathedral, Episcopal Palace and other Church property in trust for the Diocese of Toronto, and rather than betray this sacred trust we would willingly give up our lives.

ERRORS CONCERNING MODERN LIBERALISM.

Modern liberalism has also its note of censure. In Catholic countries where the Catholic religion has been for centuries recognized by the state, our Holy Father denies that it is no longer expedient that the Catholic religion shall be held as the only religion of the state to the exclusion of all other modes of worship, and, as a consequence, he also denies that it has been wisely provided by law in some countries called Catholic, that persons coming to reside therein shall enjoy the " public" exercise of their own worship.

Let us calmly consider this important question, let us view it in the light of impartial history, and we shall find no difficulty in comprehending why the Holy Father has condemned the aforesaid propositions:

Even England upholds the principles established by the condemnation of the first of these propositions, by maintaining the Anglican Established Church, as the great bulwark of the State in England and Ireland. The Pope has here only condemned indifferentism; that is to say, that religion, God, the soul, truth, virtue, the Gospel and the

Koran, Buddha, and Jesus Christ stand on equal footing, and are equally beneficial to people and nations. So the Pope could not but condemn such absurdity. Our Lord has established but one religion, and that one religion must be the best for peoples. Our Lord came not to sow divisions. He is not, therefore, their author, and consequently divisions are not the best state of things. How, then, could the Pope declare them to be so? It is absurd to assert that religious divisions can conduce to the benefit of the State. What did the religious divisions which sprung up in Europe in the sixteenth century do for the benefit of state? Were they not introduced into the various countries by fire and sword, and were not the fairest portions of Christendom desolated by the wars caused there by religious convulsions? The Pope simply says, and he is justified by history, that religious divisions are not for the benefit of the state, and no Catholic country acts wisely in introducing and "*providing by law*" for such divisions. But does he therefore condemn toleration? By no means. The Pope himself practices it at Rome. The Jews and the Protestants are free in the Eternal City. The former have their Synagogue and the latter have their temple. But, then are Protestants themselves so very tolerant in their own countries? What are the facts? Denmark, Norway and Sweden, all Protestant countries, are the most intolerant in Europe. The laws in some of these countries punish converts to Catholicism with confiscation of their property, and with exile. An instance of this occurred a short time ago in Sweden to the scandal of all Europe. Russia, with a schismatic creed, visits with the gravest punishments those who secede from the national Church. God alone knows the atrocities inflicted on the Poles to force them into the Russian Church. And what has England itself done up to a very recent date? The year of 1827 is not a very remote period. Up to that time the most odious and cruel laws of intolerance pressed heavily on the very manhood, as well as on the religion of Catholics. We spare the generous feelings of a large number of Englishmen of the present generation by abstaining from a recital of those laws. They would chafe against such quotations. In doing so, they manifest the throes of an upright conscience, which throes are but the awakenings of an angry repentance in the morning which succeeds a long night of revelry. Acts of Parliament will not be easily obliterated from a nation's memory, and history cannot be so soon forgotten. We have not as yet learned that the Popes have enacted such sanguinary laws as those on the statute books of Protestant countries. We have heard much of the Spanish Inquisition, many of whose acts were repu-

2

dinted by the Popes. But yet, we would calmly await the results of the credit and debit side of the ledger recording the laws, penalties and judgments of Catholic and Protestant countries respectively. It is true, the Pope condemns those Catholic rulers of Catholic countries who *"provide by law"* that immigrants or strangers who may come into their dominions should enjoy the *public* exercise of their various forms of worship. But here let us observe, that our Holy Father does not condemn those rulers who tolerate the various creeds of persons already resident in their country, provided that those creeds be not subversive of public morality and the peace of the realm. Would Buddhism be tolerated in England? Does it tolerate the sacrifice of widows on the tombs of their departed husbands, or the immolation of children under the wheels of the Juggernaut in India? Are there no laws against the religion of Mormon immigrants in the United States? The Pagan Chinese are at present infecting society in California with their abominable rites, and must soon be discountenanced by that State, in the interests and for the life of society. Formal error in religion is a sin as well as the well-head of many other sins and crimes.

Some non-Catholic countries are exclusive in the extreme. We were amused to read of State conversions from Protestantism to the worship of the Blessed Eucharist, veneration to the Blessed Virgin, and other doctrines, sworn against by the head of the Anglican Church, by aspirants to thrones in exclusive Greece and Russia. Our good Queen of England herself, in the exclusive creed of her State Church, has no other alternative than to lose her Crown or profess the Protestant religion. There is no note of horror or burst of indignation at the exclusiveness of those non-Catholic kingdoms; but let Rome only enunciate like principles and the case is altered. The Church never used the sword, nor brute force, nor pains or penalties to propagate her doctrine. We cannot say so much of Protestant powers.

LXXX.—The Roman Pontiff can and ought to Reconcile and Harmonise Himself with Progress, Liberalism, and Modern Civilisation.

We shall here reproduce what we have already said on this point in a lecture delivered by us in our Cathedral on the 29th January last:

"Our Holy Father in the 80th proposition, the last of the series, condemns those that say, 'The Roman Pontiff can and ought to reconcile himself to, and agree with progress, liberalism and modern civilisation.' Our Holy Father appears by condemning this proposition to give a

it the results of
aws, penalties and
pectively. It is
atholic countries
s who may come
of their various
ur Holy Father
rious creeds
hat those creeds
of the realm.
lerate the sacri-
s, or the immo-
in India? Are
s in the United
society in Cali-
iscountenanced

Formal error
other sins and

xtreme. We
tantism to the
Blessed Virgin,
glican Church,
n. Our good
State Church,
the Protestant
nation at the
t Rome only
Church never
propagate her

CONCILE AND
AND MODERN

this point in
uary last:
e series, con-
to reconcile
civilisation.'
n to give a

universal condemnation to many of the errors contained in former propositions, as well as to reprobate the specific doctrine taught in this one. The proud world in this age of universal progress and civilisation, writhes under the lash of this condemnation, and pours forth its vials of abuse and calumny on the head of its judge and condemner.

Our Holy Father does not condemn society, nor does he invite it to return to the uncouth and unpolished practices of the middle ages. He does not fear, and does not condemn the activity of the human mind in the right direction. He dreads, and suffers from ignorance, more than from honest pursuit after truth. He holds out a helping hand to science, to the arts he bids welcome; to just governments he says proceed, prosper, and rule, and to well regulated societies he says, " you are our crown and our joy," but to the evil doer, he is a terror, for he holdeth not the sword of the word of God in vain, and he reproves the liar and the boaster. Taking the Gospel for our guide, and expositor of right and wrong, as I am addressing a Christian Congregation, let us examine this 80th proposition which seems to be the most misunderstood, and also ill-interpreted. Let us settle the Pontiff's meaning as to the word " progress, liberalism, and modern civilisation," to which the Pope cannot be reconciled. Does our Holy Father want to check the world in its onward course of improvement? Does he pretend to contend with and overthrow the progressive and conquering genius and talent of the world? Will he forbid science to subject the grand elements, fire, water, and electricity, to the use and comfort of man? Does he forbid the geologist to seek deep into the secrets of nature, or study the beauteous volumes of divine creation, or the astronomer to visit the world that God has made, and tell his fellowmen the size, shape and weight, the revolutions and the changes of those heavenly bodies, which in letters of light write their creator's name on the starry skies above us? Does he wish to curb the mighty genius of man, which, under the inspiration of a kind and merciful Providence, invents new comforts for his fellow-beings, and like a second creator, puts life and motion into inanimate matter, and adapts it to his use and enjoyment? None of all this. The Roman Pontiff always protected genius. The engines of flaming fire—*ignis urens*—bring thousands of wandering voyageurs to Rome, to contemplate the new as well as the old works of art, in that centre of civilisation. The lightening of heaven too is chained there, and loosed again to flash its messages of joy or sorrow, of loss or gain throughout old Europe. Students of every taste and clime seek in Rome the perfect in the fine arts, in painting, in sculpture and in music. The college of the Propaganda with its seventy-two languages, prints the word of God, and sends it with its missionaries, well instructed in divine things, to their people of various nations and tongues. The world gives the Pope credit for introducing into his own dominions great reforms. He granted amnesty to political offenders, liberated prisoners, recalled exiles, freed the press from censorship, in a great part removed many of the disabilities of the Jews, and was preparing to have a representative Parliament, and made other advances towards real progress and true liberalism. He cannot be opposed to himself and condemn his own acts. Therefore, he cannot be opposed to real progress and true liberalism.

The meaning attached to the words progress, liberalism, and modern civilisation, in the false philosophy of the age, is, that man on earth is superior to God, human reason is superior to Divine revelation, the sacred word of God is filled with fables and lies. Philosophy or human science is superior to Theology or Divine science. Reason is deified, nay it is made superior to God and his revelation. The Providence of God does not mix up in human concerns. The world can get along without God, it must be divorced from him. His revelation is imperfect—not sufficient. Man in his pride imitates Lucifer, and proclaims himself superior to God. Our Holy Father in his zeal for the glory of his Divine Master, cries out with St. Michael, "Who is like unto God?" and condemns these flagrant errors.

Should we not, beloved Brethren, "glory in such a Pontiff," now in his seventy-third year. Young in heart, clear in mind, vigorous in intellect, calm amidst the storm, confiding in the presence of God and in is guiding star Mary, blessing those who curse him, praying for those who persecute him, and winning by his tender personal piety and benign and heavenly countenance all hearts. God raises up great men in his Church to do great things, and to breast great storms, and for great and difficult contingencies. Such a man is our Holy Father. He has lived longer as head of the Church than 250 out of the 259 Popes who have governed the Church ; he has delivered more homilies, allocutions, written more pastoral letters, and canonized more saints than most of his predecessors. He erected more archiepiscopal sees throughout the world than had been established for hundreds of years previously, and what he, as well as the whole world, considers the grand act of his Pontificate, the Dogmatical definition of the Immaculate Conception is his crown, his glory, his honor and his protection. We rejoice, therefore, in revering him as head of the Catholic Church, and the representative of Christ on earth. We receive from his infallible teaching all truths. Christ said to Peter, and "Thou being once converted, confirm thy brethren (Luc. xxii. 32).

The Popes — successors of Peter — confirm their brethren of the Episcopacy in those doctrines and truths of which that body in conjunction with their head, the Supreme Pontiff is the depository and expounder.

CONDITIONS OF THE JUBILEE.

It only remains for us now, beloved Brethren, to indicate to you the conditions upon which the indulgences granted in the Jubilee are to be obtained.

The plenary indulgence granted in the Jubilee is a remission of the temporal punishment due to sin after they have been remitted in the Sacrament of penance. Hence, a good confession, with a sincere repentance and an entire change of the heart to God, is the first condition of gaining the indulgences of the Jubilee. "Be ye therefore converted to me with all your heart, in fasting, in weeping, and in mourning" (Joel, ii. 12) ; "If we confess our sins He is faithful and just to forgive us our sins and to cleanse us from all iniquity" (Epis. St. John, i. 9). The second condition is a good communion, "Unless you eat the flesh of the Son of Man and drink his blood you shall not have life in you" (John vi. 54). The third condition is to fast on Wednesday, Friday and Saturday of one week during the month of the Jubilee. "Prayer is good with fasting and alms more than to lay up treasures of gold" (Tobias xii. 8). Confessors may commute to other good works this condition in favor of those who are not able to fast.

Fourth condition, alms deeds, "Redeem thou thy sins with alms and thy iniquities with works of mercy to the poor" (Daniel iv. 24). "Alms delivereth from death, and the same is that which purgeth away sins and maketh to find life everlasting" (Tobias xii. 9). Let the rich give abundantly and the poor according to their means. We designate the House of Providence and the Industrial School at St. Mary's as the best objects of charity to receive such alms. We request the Parish Priests to have " *Jubilee alms boxes* " in each of their Churches, and to forward the sums received to our Chancellor for distribution.

Fifth. Three visits to the Parish Church in the country; and one visit to three Churches in the city, viz., our Cathedral of St. Michael, St. Mary's of the Immaculate Conception, and St. Paul's. At each visit earnest prayers are to be offered to God for the intentions of our Holy Father, which we have enumerated in the commencement of our pastoral. That is to say : the conversion of sinners, heretics, infidels, and schismatics, the welfare and protection of the Sovereign Pontiff, the extension of our holy faith, justice and peace amongst rulers and princes of the earth, and that the scourges of war, famine and pestilence may be removed from us. Five O... Father's, and five Hail Mary's, will suffice for these intentions. "Ask and it shall be given to you, seek and you shall find, knock and it shall be opened to you" (Luke, xi. 9).

We appoint the time from the thirteenth Sunday after Pentecost, the 3rd of September, to Tuesday, 3rd of October, as the time wherein shall be held the Jubilee in the rural parishes of our Diocese. For the city of Toronto we appoint the month of November.

The Jubilee which has been proclaimed, beloved Brethren, will prove, I hope, as others have, that the "Mercy of God is from generation to generation, to them that fear Him" (Luc. i. 50); that His grace being poured out "All flesh shall see the salvation of God" (Luc. iii. 3). Hard hearts will be softened to repentance, the weak strengthened, the tempted succoured, the indifferent aroused, and the just made more just. "The Lord shall feed his flock as a Shepherd; He shall gather together the lambs with his arms, He shall take them up to his bosom" (Isaiah, 40). How many sinners, like the Prodigal Son, who are now starving on the husks of swine, the filth of sin, will return to their Father's house, and cry out and say, "Father, I have sinned against Heaven, and before thee, I am now unworthy to be called Thy son" (Luc. xv.). The compassionate and indulgent Father of all mercy will receive his penitent child to his paternal heart, "Many sins will be forgiven him because he loved much." He will be clothed with the white garment of grace, and he will be made sit down, not merely to the supper of fatted calf, but to the celestial banquet of our Lord's body and blood.

"Blessed are your eyes because they see, and your ears because they hear, amen; for I say unto you, many prophets and just men have desired to see the things that you see, and have not seen them, and to hear the things that you hear and have not heard them." (Math. xiii.)

Miracles of grace and mercy will be witnessed, and men and "angels will rejoice."

Your devoted clergy, beloved Brethren, in the ardor of their zeal to fulfil the first duty and most anxious desire of their sacerdotal piety, conceived in early life, will rejoice to be to you the kind and indulgent Father, in imitation of Him whose ministers they are and whose graces they dispense to you. (1 Cor. iv.)

Our own heart, often depressed by the apprehension of the rigorous account to be rendered to the Sovereign Judge of your souls (Heb. xiii.) will be comforted, and our anxiety alleviated, and will rejoice in the universal joy of Jubilee, in the well grounded hope, and almost conviction, that all our beloved children in Christ will profit by those days of mercy and grace.

There may be some who will refuse and reject these proferred graces, as even in the days of our Lord Jesus Christ some were found. He said to his eternal Father, "Those whom thou gavest me I have kept, and none of them hath perished, except the son of perdition" (John iii. 17). God grant, dearly beloved Brethren, that there be no sons of perdition amongst you. Let us again exhort you to profit of the mercy of God here that you may rejoice with him in eternity. Pray with confidence to the Immaculate Mother of God, who has maternal influence with her Divine Son, and whose pure prayers will obtain for us what our unworthiness would hardly dare ask.

The grace of our Lord Jesus Christ, and the charity of God, and the communication of the Holy Spirit be with you all. Amen.

JOHN JOSEPH,
Bishop of Toronto.

Given at St. Michael's Palace, Toronto, on the Feast of Corpus Christi, June 15, in the year of our Lord 1865.

This Pastoral shall be read in all the Churches of the Diocese, on the first Sunday after its reception.

☞ As several imperfect or faulty English translations of the Encyclical Letter of the Pope, and of its Annex, or *Syllabus* of errors condemned, have been published, it has been thought expedient to republish both documents, in a version which has been carefully revised and compared with the original, and which may therefore be regarded as substantially correct and authentic. We take the translation from the illustrious Archbishop of Baltimore.

THE ENCYCLICAL OF POPE PIUS IX.

PIUS PP. IX.

To Our Venerable Brothers, the Patriarchs, Primates, Archbishops and Bishops, of the Universal Church, having Grace and Communion with the Apostolic See.

HEALTH AND APOSTOLIC BENEDICTION:

It is well known unto all men, and especially to You, Venerable Brothers, with what great care and pastoral vigilance our Predecessors, the Roman Pontiffs, have discharged the Office entrusted by Christ our Lord to them, in the Person of the Most Blessed Peter, Prince of the Apostles, have unremittingly discharged the duty of feeding the lambs and the sheep, and have diligently nourished the Lord's entire flock with the words of faith, imbued it with salutary doctrine, and guarded it from poisoned pastures. And those our Predecessors, who were the assertors and Champions of the august Catholic Religion, of faith and justice, being as they were chiefly solicitous for the salvation of souls, held nothing to be of so great importance as the duty of exposing and condemning, in their most wise Letters and Constitutions, all heresies and errors, which are hostile to moral honesty and to the eternal salvation of mankind, and which have frequently stirred up terrible commotions, and have damaged both the Christian and civil commonwealths in a disastrous manner. Wherefore those our Predecessors have, with Apostolic fortitude, continually resisted the machinations of those evil men, who, "foaming out their own confusion, like the raging waves of the sea," and "promising liberty, while they are themselves the slaves of corruption," endeavored by their fallacious opinions and most wicked writings to subvert the foundations of Religion and of civil Society, to remove from our midst all virtue and justice, to deprave the hearts and minds of all, to turn away from right discipline of morals the incautious, and especially inexperienced youth, miserably corrupting them, leading them into the nets of error, and finally withdrawing them from the bosom of the Catholic Church.

And now, Venerable Brothers, as is also very well known to you, scarcely had We (by the secret dispensation of Divine Providence, certainly by no merit of Our own) been called to this Chair of Peter, when We, to the extreme grief of Our soul, beheld a horrible tempest, stirred up by so many erroneous opinions, and the dreadful and never enough to be lamented mischiefs which redound to Christian people from such errors; and We then, in discharge of Our Apostolic Ministerial Office, imitating the example of Our illustrious Predecessors, raised Our voice, and in several published Encyclical Letters, and in Allocutions delivered in Consistory, and in other Apostolical Letters, We condemned the prominent, most grievous errors of the age, and We stirred up your excellent episcopal vigilance, and again and again did we admonish and exhort all the sons of the Catholic Church, who are most dear to Us, that they should abhor and shun all the said errors, as they would the contagion of a fatal pestilence. Especially in Our first Encyclical Letter, written to You on the 9th of November, A. D. 1846, and in two Allocutions, one of which was delivered by Us in Consistory on the 9th of December, A. D. 1854, and the other on the 9th of June, A. D. 1862, We condemned the monstrous and portentous opinions, which prevail especially in the present age, to the very great loss of souls, and even to the detriment of civil society, and which are in the highest degree hostile, not only to the Catholic Church, and to her salutary doctrine and venerable laws, but also to the everlasting law of nature engraven by God upon the hearts of all men, and to right reason; and out of which almost all errors originate.

Now although hitherto We have not omitted to denounce and reprove the chief errors of this kind, yet the cause of the Catholic Church and the salvation of souls committed to us by God, and even the interests of human society, absolutely demand, that once again we should stir up your pastoral solicitude, to drive away other erroneous opinions which flow from those errors above specified, as their source. These false and perverse opinions are so much the more detestable, by as much as they have chiefly for their object to hinder and banish that salutary influence which the Catholic Church, by the institution and command of her Divine Author, ought freely to exercise, even to the consummation of the world, not only over individual men, but over nations, peoples, and sovereigns, and to abolish that mutual co-operation and agreement of counsels between the Priesthood and Governments, which has always been propitious and conducive to the welfare both of Church and State. (Gregory XVI. Encyclical, 13th August, 1832.) For you know well, Venerable Brethren, that at this time there are found not a few, who, applying to civil intercourse the impious and absurd principles of what they call *Naturalism*, dare teach, "that the best form of Society, and the exigencies of civil progress, absolutely require human society to be constituted and governed without any regard whatsoever to Religion; as if this (Religion) did not even exist, or at least without making any distinction between true and false religions." Contrary to the teaching of the Holy Scriptures, of the Church, and of the Holy Fathers, these persons do not hesitate to assert, that "the best condition of human society is that, wherein no duty is recognized by the Government of correcting, by enacted penalties, the violators of the Catholic Religion, except when the maintenance of the public peace requires it." From this totally false notion of social government, they fear not to uphold that erroneous opinion, most pernicious to the Catholic Church, and to the salvation of souls, which was called by Our Predecessor Gregory XVI. (lately quoted) an insanity (delirimentum), (Encycl. 13 August, 1832): namely, "that the liberty of conscience and of worship is the peculiar (or inalienable) right of every man, which should be proclaimed by law, and that citizens have the right to all kinds of liberty, to be restrained by no law, whether ecclesiastical or civil, by which they may be enabled to manifest openly and publicly their ideas, by word of mouth, through the press, or by any other means." But whilst these men make these rash assertions, they do not reflect, or consider, that they preach the liberty of perdition (St. Augustine, Epistle 105, al. 166), and that, "if it is always free to human arguments to discuss, men will never be wanting who will dare to resist the truth, and to rely upon the loquacity of human wisdom, when we know from the command of our Lord Jesus Christ, how faith and Christian wisdom ought to avoid this most mischievous vanity." (St. Leo, Epistle 164, al. 133, sec. 2, Boll. ed.)

And since Religion has been excluded from civil Society, and the doctrine and authority of Divine Revelation, or the true and germane notion of justice and human right have been obscured and lost, and material or brute force substituted in the place of true justice and legitimate right, it is easy to perceive why some persons, forgetting and trampling upon the most certain principles of sound reason, dare cry out together, "that the will of the people, manifested by what they call public opinion, or in any other way, constitutes the supreme law, independent of all divine and human right, and that, in the political order, accomplished facts, by the mere fact of having been accomplished, have the force of right." But who does not see and plainly understand that the society of man, freed from the bonds of religion and of true justice, can certainly have no other purpose than the effort to obtain and accumulate wealth, and that in its actions it follows no other law than that of the uncurbed cupidity which seeks to secure its own pleasures and comforts? For this reason also, these same men persecute with such bitter hatred the Religious Orders, who have deserved so well of Religion, Civil Society and Letters; they loudly declare that these Orders have no right to exist, and, in so doing, make common cause with the falsehoods of the heretics. For, as was most wisely taught by Our Predecessor of illustrious memory, Pius VI., "the abolition of Religious Orders injures the state of public profession of the Evangelical Counsels; injures a mode of life recommended by the Church, as in conformity with Apostolical doctrine; does wrong to the illustrious founders whom we venerate upon our altars, and who constituted these societies under the inspiration of God." (Epistle to Cardinal de la Rochefaucauld, March 10, 1791.)

And these same persons also impiously pretend, that citizens should be deprived of the liberty of publicly bestowing on the Church their alms for the sake of Christian charity, and that the law forbidding "servile labour on account of Divine worship" upon certain fixed days should be abolished, upon the most fallacious pretext that such liberty and such law are contrary to the principles of political economy. Not content with abolishing Religion in public society, they desire further to banish it from families and private life. Teaching and professing those most fatal errors of Socialism and Communism, they declare that "domestic society, or the family, derives all its reason of existence solely from civil law, whence it is to be concluded that from civil law descend and depend all the rights of parents over their children, and, above all, the right of instructing and educating them." By such impious opinions and machinations do these false teachers endeavour to eliminate the salutary teaching and influence of the Catholic Church from the instruction and education of youth, and miserably to infect and deprave by every pernicious error and vice the tender and pliant minds of youth. All those who endeavour to throw into confusion both religious and political affairs, to destroy the good order of society, and to annihilate all divine and human rights, have always exerted all their criminal schemes, attention and efforts upon the manner in which they might, above all, deprave and delude unthinking youth, as we have already shown: it is upon the corruption of youth that they place all their hopes. Thus they never cease to attack by every method the Clergy, both secular and regular, from whom, as testify to us in so conspicuous a manner the most certain records of history, such considerable benefits have been bestowed in abundance upon Christian and civil society, and upon the republic of Letters; asserting of the Clergy in general, that they are the enemies of the useful sciences, of progress, and of civilization, and that they ought to be deprived of all participation in the work of teaching and training the young.

Others, reviving the depraved fictions of innovators, errors many times condemned, presume, with extraordinary impudence, to subordinate the authority of the Church and of this Apostolic See, conferred upon it by Christ Our Lord, to the judgment of civil authority, and to deny all the rights of this same Church and this See with regard to those things which appertain to the secular order. For these persons do not blush to affirm, " that the laws of the Church do not bind the conscience, if they are not promulgated by the civil power; that the acts and decrees of the Roman Pontiffs concerning religion and the Church require the sanction and approbation, or at least the assent of the civil power; and that the Apostolic Constitutions, (Clement XII., Benedict XIV., Pius VII., Leo XII.) condemning secret societies, whether these exact or do not exact an oath of secrecy, and branding with anathema their followers and partizans, have no force in those countries of the world where such associations are tolerated by the civil Government." It is likewise affirmed, " that the excommunications launched by the Council of Trent and the Roman Pontiffs against those who invade and usurp the possessions of the Church and its rights, strive, by confounding the spiritual and temporal orders, to attain solely a mere earthly end; that the Church can decide nothing which may bind the consciences of the faithful in the temporal order of things; that the right of the Church is not competent to restrain with temporal penalties the violaters of her laws; and that it is in accordance with the principles of theology and of public law, for the civil Government to appropriate property possessed by the Churches, the Religious Orders, and other pious establishments." And they have no shame in avowing openly and publicly the heretical statement and principle, from which have emanated so many errors and perverse opinions, " that the ecclesiastical power is not, by the law of God, made distinct from and independent of the civil power, and that no distinction, no independence of this kind can be maintained without the Church invading and usurping the essential rights of the civil power." Neither can we pass over in silence the audacity of those who, not enduring sound doctrine, assert that "the judgments and decrees of the Holy See, the object of which is declared to concern the general welfare of the Church, its rights and its discipline, do not claim acqui- escence and obedience, under pain of sin and loss of the Catholic pro- fession, if they do not treat of the dogmas of faith and of morals."

How contrary is this doctrine to the Catholic dogma, of the plenary power divinely conferred on the Roman Pontiff by our Lord Jesus Christ, to guide, to supervise and to govern the Universal Church, no one can fail to see and understand, clearly and evidently.

Amid so great a diversity of depraved opinions. We, remembering Our Apostolic duty, and solicitous before all things for Our most holy Religion, for sound doctrine, for the salvation of the souls confided to Us, and for the welfare of human Society itself, have considered the moment opportune to raise anew Our Apostolic voice. Therefore do We, by Our Apostolic authority, reprobate, denounce and condemn generally and particularly all the evil opinions and doctrines specially mentioned in this Letter, and We wish that they may be held as re- probated, denounced and condemned by all the children of the Catholic Church.

But You know further, Venerable Brothers, that in Our time the haters of all truth and justice, and violent enemies of our Religion have spread abroad other impious doctrines, by means of pestilent books, pamphlets, and journals, which, distributed over the surface of the earth, deceive the people and wickedly lie. You are not ignorant that in our day men are found who, animated and excited by the spirit of Satan, have arrived at that excess of impiety as not to fear to deny Our Lord and Master Jesus Christ, and to attack His Divinity with scandalous persistence. And here We cannot abstain from awarding You well-merited praise, Venerable Brothers, for all the care and zeal, with which You have raised Your episcopal voice against so great an impiety.

And therefore in this present Letter, We speak to You with all affection ; to You who, called to partake Our cares, are Our greatest support in the midst of Our very great grief ; Our joy and consolation, by reason of the excellent piety of which You give proof in maintain- ing Religion, and the marvellous love, faith, and discipline with which, united by the strongest and most affectionate ties to Us and this Apos- tolic See, You strive valiantly and accurately to fulfil Your most

ntained without
hts of the civil
ty of those who,
its and decrees
ern the general
ot claim acqui-
e Catholic pro-
of morals."
of the plenary
ur Lord Jesus
al Church, no

remembering
Our most holy
ls confided to
onsidered the
Therefore do
and condemn
ines specially
e held as re-
the Catholic

Our time the
ur Religion
of pestilent
e surface of
ot ignorant
y the spirit
ear to deny
vinity with
awarding
and zeal,
great au

with all
greatest
nsolation,
maintain-
h which,
is Apos-
ur most

weighty episcopal ministry. We do then expect, from Your excellent pastoral zeal, that, taking the sword of the Spirit, which is the Word of God, and strengthened by the grace of Our Lord Jesus Christ, You will watch with redoubled care, that the faithful committed to Your charge "abstain from evil pasturage, which Jesus Christ doth not till, because His Father hath not planted it." (St. Ignatius, M. ad Philadelph. St. Leo, Epist. 156, al 125.) Never cease, then, to inculcate on the faithful that all true happiness for mankind proceeds from our august Religion, from its doctrine and practice, and that that people is happy who have the Lord for their God (Psalm 143.) Teach them, "that kingdoms rest upon the foundations of the Catholic faith (St. Celest, Epist. 22 ad. Syn. Eph.), and that nothing is so deadly, nothing so certain to engender every ill, nothing so exposed to danger, as for men to believe that they stand in need of nothing else than the free will which we received at birth, if we ask nothing further from the Lord; that is to say, if, forgetting our Author, we abjure His power to show that we are free." And do not omit to teach, "that the royal power has been established, not only to exercise the government of the world, but, above all, for the protection of the Church (St. Leo, Epist. 156, al. 125); and that there is nothing more profitable and more glorious for the Sovereigns of States, and Kings, than to leave the Catholic Church to exercise her laws, and not to permit any to curtail her liberty;" as Our most wise and courageous Predecessor, St. Felix, wrote to the Emperor Zeno. "It is certain that it is advantageous for Sovereigns, when the cause of God is in question, to submit their Royal will, according to his ordinance, to the Priests of Jesus Christ, and not to prefer it before them." (Pius VII. Epist., Encycl, *Diu satis*, 15th May, 1800.)

And if always, so especially at present, Venerable Brothers, in the midst of the numerous calamities of the Church and of civil Society, in view also of the terrible conspiracy of our adversaries against the Catholic Church and this Apostolic See, and the great accumulation of errors, it is before all things necessary to go with faith to the Throne of Grace, to obtain mercy and find Grace in timely aid. We have therefore judged it right to excite the piety of all the faithful, in order that, with Us and with You all, they may pray without ceasing to the Father of lights and of mercies, supplicating and beseeching Him fervently and humbly, and in the plenitude of their faith they may seek refuge in Our Lord Jesus Christ, who has redeemed us to God with His blood, that by their earnest and continual prayers, they may obtain from that most dear Heart, victim of burning charity for us, that it would draw all to Himself by the bonds of His love, that all men being inflamed by His holy love may live according to His heart, pleasing God in all things, and being fruitful in all good works.

But, as there is no doubt that the prayers most agreeable to God, are those of men who approach Him with a heart pure from all stain, We have thought it good to open to Christians, with Apostolic liberality, the heavenly treasures of the Church confided to Our dispensation, so that the faithful, more strongly drawn towards true piety, and purified from the stain of their sins by the Sacrament of Penance, may more confidently offer up their prayers to God and obtain His mercy and grace.

By these Letters therefore, emanating from Our Apostolic authority, We grant to all and each of the faithful of both sexes throughout the Catholic world a Plenary Indulgence, in the manner of a Jubilee, during one month, up to the end of the coming year 1865, and not longer, to be carried into effect by You, Venerable Brethren, and the other legitimate local Ordinaries, in the form and manner laid down at the commencement of Our Sovereign Pontificate by Our Apostolical Letters, in form of a brief, dated the 20th of November, A. D. 1846, and sent to the whole Episcopate of the world, commencing with the words, *"Arcano Divinæ Providentiæ consilio,"* and with the faculties given by Us in those same Letters. We desire, however, that all the prescriptions of Our Letters shall be observed, saving the exceptions We have declared are to be made. And We have granted this, notwithstanding all which might make to the contrary, even those worthy of special and individual mention and derogation; and in order that every doubt and difficulty may be removed, We have ordered that copies of those Letters should be again forwarded to You.

Let us implore, Venerable Brethren, from our inmost hearts, and with all our souls, the mercy of God. He has encouraged us so to do, by saying: "I will not withdraw My mercy from them." "Let us ask and we shall receive; and if there is slowness or delay in the reception, because we have grievously offended, let us knock, because to him that knocketh it shall be opened; if our prayers, groans, and tears, in which we must persist and be obstinate, knock at the door: and if our prayers be united; let each one pray to God, not for himself alone, but for all his brethren, as the Lord hath taught us to pray." (St. Cyprian, Epistle 11.) But, in order that God may accede more easily to our and your prayers, and to those of all His faithful servants, let us employ in all confidence, as our Mediatrix with Him, the Virgin Mary, Mother of God, who " has destroyed all heresies throughout the world, and who, the most loving Mother of us all, is very gracious . . . and full of mercy, ... allows herself to be entreated by all, shows herself most clement towards all, and takes under her pitying care all our necessities with a most ample affection," (*St. Bernard, Serm de duodecim prærogativis B. V. M. in verbis Apocalyp.*;) and, "sitting as queen at the right hand of her only begotten Son, Our Lord Jesus Christ, in a golden vestment clothed around with various adornments," there is nothing which she cannot obtain from Him. Let us implore also the intervention of the Blessed Peter, Chief of the Apostles, and of his co-Apostle Paul, and of all those Saints of Heaven, who, having already become the friends of God, have been admitted into the celestial kingdom, where they are crowned and bear palms in their hands; and who, henceforth certain of their own immortality, are solicitous for our salvation.

In conclusion, we ask of God from our inmost soul the abundance of all His celestial benefits for you, and we bestow upon you, Venerable Brethren, and upon all the faithful Clergy and Laity committed to your care, Our Apostolic Benediction from the most loving depths of Our heart, in token of Our charity toward you.

PIUS, PP. IX.

Given at Rome, from St. Peter's, this 8th day of December, 1864, the tenth anniversary of the Dogmatic Definition of the Immaculate Conception of the Virgin Mary, Mother of God, in the nineteenth year of Our Pontificate.

THE SYLLABUS

Of the Principal Errors of our Time, which are Stigmatized in the Consistorial Allocutions, Encyclical, and other Apostolical Letters of Our Most Holy Father, Pope Pius IX.

Section I. — Pantheism, Naturalism, and Absolute Rationalism.

I. There exists no Divine Power, Supreme Being, Wisdom, and Providence distinct from the universe, and God is none other than nature, and is therefore mutable. In effect, God is produced in man and in the world, and all things are God, and have the very substance of God. God is therefore one and the same thing with the world, and thence spirit is the same thing with matter, necessity with liberty, true with false, good with evil, justice with injustice. (Allocution *Maxima quidem*, 9th June, 1862.)

II. All action of God upon man and the world is to be denied. (Allocution *Maxima quidem*, 9th June, 1862.)

III. Human reason, without any regard to God, is the sole arbiter of truth and falsehood, of good and evil; it is its own law to itself, and suffices by its natural force to secure the welfare of men and of nations. (Allocution *Maxima quidem*, 9th June, 1862.)

IV. All the truths of Religion are derived from the native strength of human reason; whence reason is the master rule by which man can and ought to arrive at the knowledge of all truths of every kind. (Encyclical letters, *Qui Pluribus*, 9th November, 1846, *Singulari quidem*, 17th March, 1856, and the Allocution *Maxima quidem*, 9th June, 1862.)

V. Divine revelation is imperfect, and, therefore, subject to a continual and indefinite progress, which corresponds with the progress of human reason. Encyclical *Qui Pluribus*, 9th November, 1846, and the Allocution *Maxima quidem*, 9th June, 1862.)

VI. Christian faith is in opposition to human reason, and divine revelation not only does not benefit, but even injures the perfection of man. (Encyclical *Qui Pluribus*, 9th November, 1846, and the Allocution *Maxima quidem*, 9th June, 1862.)

VII. The prophecies and miracles uttered and narrated in the Sacred Scriptures, are the fictions of poets; and the mysteries of the Christian faith, the result of philosophical investigations. In the books of the two testaments there are contained mythical inventions, and Jesus Christ is Himself a mythical fiction. (Encyclical *Qui pluribus*, 9th November, 1846, and the Allocution *Maxima quidem*, 9th June, 1862.)

Section II.—Moderate Rationalism.

VIII. As human reason is placed on a level with Religion, so theological matters must be treated in the same manner as philosophical ones. (Allocution *Singulari quadem perfusi*, 9th December, 1854.)

IX. All the dogmas of the Christian Religion are, without exception, the object of natural science or philosophy, and human reason, instructed solely by history, is able, by its own natural strength and principles, to arrive at the true knowledge of even the most abstruse dogmas; *provided* such dogmas be proposed as subject matter for human reason. (Letter to the Archbishop Frising. *Gravissimas*, 11th December, 1862—to the same, *Tuas libenter*, 21st December, 1863.)

X. As the philosopher is one thing, and philosophy is another, so it is the right and duty of the philosopher to submit himself to the authority which he shall have recognized as true; but philosophy neither can, nor ought to submit to any authority. (Letter to Archbishop Frising. *Gravissimas*, 11th December, 1862—to the same, *Tuas libenter*, 21st December, 1863.)

XI. The Church not only ought never to animadvert upon philosophy, but ought to tolerate the errors of philosophy, leaving to philosophy the care of their correction. (Letter to Archbishop Frising, 11th December, 1862.)

XII. The decrees of the Apostolic See and of the Roman Congregation fetter the free progress of science. (Id. Ibid.)

XIII. The method and principles, by which the old scholastic Doctors cultivated theology, are no longer suitable to the demands of the age and the progress of science. (Ib. Tuas libenter, 21st December, 1863.)

XIV. Philosophy must be treated of without any account being taken of supernatural revelation. (Id. Ibid.)

N.B.—To the rationalistic system belong, in great part, the errors of Anthony Gunther, condemned in the letter to the Cardinal Archbishop of Cologne, "*Eximiam tuam*," June 15, 1847; and in that to the Bishop of Breslau, "*Dolore haud mediocri*," April 30, 1860.)

Section III.—Indifferentism, Latitudinarianism.

XV. Every man is free to embrace and profess the Religion he shall believe true, guided by the light of reason. (Apostolic Letters Multiplices inter. 10th June, 1851. Allocution Maxima quidem, 9th June, 1862.)

XVI. Men may in any religion find the way of eternal salvation, and obtain eternal salvation. (Encyclical letter Qui pluribus, 9th November, 1846. Allocution, Ubi primum, 17th December, 1847. Encyclical letter Singulari quidem, 17th March, 1856.)

XVII. We may entertain at least a well founded hope for the eternal salvation of all those, who are in no manner in the true Church of Christ. (Allocution Singulari quadem, 9th December, 1854. Encyclical letter Quanto conficiamur, 17th August, 1863.)

XVIII. Protestantism is nothing more than another form of the same true Christian Religion, in which it is possible to be equally pleasing to God as in the Catholic Church. (Encyclical letter Noscitis et nobiscum, 8th December, 1849.)

Section IV.—Socialism, Communism, Secret Societies, Biblical Societies Clerico-Liberal Locutier.

Pests of this description are frequently rebuked in the severest terms in the Encyc. *Qui pluribus*, November 9, 1846 ; Alloc. *Quibus quantis pw*, August 20, 1849 ; Encyc. *Noscitis et Nobiscum*, December 8, 1849 ; Alloc. *Singulari quadem*, December 8, 1851; Encyc. *Quanto conficiamur macrore*, August 10, 1863.

Section V.—Errors Concerning the Church and Her Rights.

XIX. The Church is not a true, and perfect, and entirely free society, nor does she enjoy peculiar and perpetual rights conferred upon her by her Divine Founder, but it appertains to the civil power to define what are the rights and limits within which the Church may exercise authority. Allocution Singulari quadem, 9th December, 1854, Multis gravibusque, 17th December, 1860, Maxima quidem, 9th June, 1862.)

XX. The ecclesiastical power must not exercise its authority without the permission and assent of the civil Government. (Allocution, Meminit unusquisque, 30th September. 1861)

XXI. The Church has not the power of defining dogmatically, that the Religion of the Catholic Church is the only true Religion. (Apostolic Letters Multiplices inter. 10th June, 1851.)

XXII. The obligation which binds Catholic teachers and authors applies only to those things which are proposed for universal belief as dogmas of the faith, by the infallible judgment of the Church. (Letters to Archbishop Frising. Tuas libenter, 21st December, 1863.)

XXIII. The Roman Pontiffs and Œcumenical Councils have exceeded the limits of their power, have usurped the rights of Princes, and have even committed errors in defining matters of faith and morals. (Apost. letter, Multiplices inter, 10th June, 1851.)

XXIV. The Church has not the power of availing herself of force, or any direct or indirect temporal power. (Letter Apost. Ad. Apostolicæ, 22nd August, 1851.)

XXV. In addition to the authority inherent in the Episcopate, a further and temporal power is granted to it by the civil authority, either expressly or tacitly, which power is on that account also revocable by the civil authority whenever it pleases. (Letter Apost. Ad. Apostolicæ, 22nd August, 1851.)

XXVI. The Church has not the innate and legitimate right of acquisition and possession. (Allocution Nunquam fore, 18th December, 1856. Encyclical Incredibili, 17th December, 1863.)

XXVII. The ministers of the Church and the Roman Pontiff ought to be absolutely excluded from all charge and dominion over temporal affairs. (Allocution Maxima quidem, 9th June, 1862.)

XXVIII. Bishops have not the right of promulgating even the Apostolical letters, without the permission of the Government. (Allocution Nunquam fore, 15th December, 1856.)

XXIX. Dispensations granted by the Roman Pontiff must be considered null, unless they have been asked for by the civil Government. (Id. Ibid.)

XXX. The immunity of the Church and of ecclesiastical persons derives its origin from civil law. (Apost. Multiplices inter, 10th June, 1851.)

XXXI. Ecclesiastical *Courts* for the temporal causes of the clergy, whether civil or criminal, ought by all means to be abolished, even without the concurrence and against the protest of the Holy See. (Allocution Acerbissimum, 27th September, 1852. And. Nunquam fore, 15th December, 1856.)

XXXII. The personal immunity exonerating the clergy from military service may be abolished, without violation either of natural right or of equity. Its abolition is called for by civil progress, especially in a community constituted upon principles of Liberal Government.

(Letter to the Archbishop of Montreal, Singularis nobisque, 29th September, 1864.)

XXXIII. It does not appertain exclusively to ecclesiastical jurisdiction, by any right proper and inherent, to direct the teaching of theological subjects. (Letter to Archbishop Frising. Tuas libenter, 21st December, 1863.)

XXXIV. The teaching of those, who compare the Sovereign Pontiff to a free Sovereign acting in the Universal Church, is a doctrine which prevailed in the Middle Ages. (Letter Apost. Ad. Apostolicæ, 22nd August, 1851.)

XXXV. There would be no obstacle to the sentence of a General Council, or the act of all the universal peoples, transferring the Pontiffical Sovereignty from the Bishop and city of Rome to some other bishopric and some other city. (Id. Ibid.)

XXXVI. The definition of a National Council does not admit of any subsequent discussion, and the civil power can regard as settled an affair decided by such National Council. (Id. Ibid.)

XXXVII. National Churches can be established, after being withdrawn and plainly separated from the authority of the Roman Pontiff. (Allocution Multis gravibusque, 17th December, 1860. Jamdudum cernimus, 18th March, 1861.)

XXXVIII. Roman Pontiffs have, by their too arbitrary conduct, contributed to the division of the Church into Eastern and Western. (Letter Apost. Ad. Apostolicæ, 22nd August, 1851.)

SECTION VI. — ERRORS ABOUT CIVIL SOCIETY, CONSIDERED BOTH IN ITSELF AND IN ITS RELATION TO THE CHURCH.

XXXIX. The state-right is the origin and source of all rights, and possesses rights which are not circumscribed by any limits. (Allocution Maxima quidem, 9th June, 1862.)

XL. The teaching of the Catholic Church is opposed to the well-being and interests of society. (Encyclical Qui pluribus, 9th November, 1846, Allocution Quibus quantisque, 20th April, 1849.)

XLI. The Civil power, even when exercised by an infidel Sovereign, possesses an indirect and negative power over religious affairs. It, therefore, possesses not only the right called that of *exequatur*, but that of the (so-called) *appelatio ab abusu*.* (Apostolic Letter, Ad. 22nd August, 1851.)

---

* The power of authorizing official acts of the Papal power, and of correcting the alleged abuses of the same.

XLII. In the case of conflicting laws between the two Powers, the civil law ought to prevail. (Letter Apost. Ad. Apostolicæ, 22nd August, 1851.)

XLIII. The civil power has a right to break, and to declare and render null the conventions (commonly called Concordats), concluded with the Apostolic See, relative to the use of rights appertaining to the ecclesiastical immunity, without the consent of the Holy See, and even contrary to its protest. (Allocution in consistoriali, 1st November, 1850. Multis gravibusque, 17th December, 1861.)

XLIV. The civil authority may interfere in matters relating to Religion, morality, and spiritual government. Hence it has control over the instructions for the guidance of consciences issued, conformably with their mission, by the Pastors of the Church. Further, it possesses power to decree, in the matter of administering the divine Sacraments, as to the dispositions necessary for their reception. (Allocution in Consistoriali, 1st November, 1850. Allocution Maxima quidem, 9th June, 1862.)

XLV. The entire direction of public schools, in which the youth of Christian States are educated, except (to a certain extent) in the case of Episcopal Seminaries, may and must appertain to the civil power, and belong to it so far, that no other authority whatsoever shall be recognized as having any right to interfere in the discipline of the schools, the arrangement of the studies, the taking of degrees, or the choice and approval of the teachers. (Allocution in Consistoriali, 1st November, 1850. Allocution Quibus luctuosissimis, 5th September, 1851.)

XLVI. Much more, even in Clerical Seminaries, the method of study to be adopted is subject to the civil authority. (Allocution Nunquam fore, 15th December, 1856.)

XLVII. The best theory of civil society requires, that popular schools open to the children of all classes, and, generally, all public institutes intended for instruction in literature and philosophy, and for conducting the education of the young, should be freed from all ecclesiastical authority, government, and interference, and should be fully subjected to the civil and political power, in conformity with the will of rulers and the prevalent opinions of the age. (Letter to the Archbishop of Fribourg, Quam non sine, 14th July, 1864.)

XLVIII. That system of instructing youth, which consists in separating it from the Catholic faith and from the power of the Church, and in teaching exclusively, or at least primarily, the knowledge of natural things and the earthly ends of social life alone, may be approved by Catholics. (Id. Ibid.)

XLIX. The civil power has the right to prevent ministers of religion and the faithful, from communicating freely and mutually with each other, and with the Roman Pontiff. (Allocution Maxima quidem, 9th June, 1862.)

L. The secular authority possesses, as inherent in itself, the right of presenting Bishops, and may require of them that they take possession of their dioceses, before having received canonical institution and the Apostolical letters from the Holy See. (Allocution Nunquam fore, 15th December, 1856.)

LI. And further, the secular Government has the right of deposing Bishops from their Pastoral functions, and it is not bound to obey the Roman Pontiff, in those things which relate to Episcopal Sees and the institution of Bishops. (Letter Apost. Multiplices inter, 10th June, 1851. Allocution, Acerbissimum, 28th September, 1852.)

LII. The Government has of itself the right to alter the age prescribed by the Church for the religious profession, both of men and women; and it may enjoin upon all religious establishments, to admit no person to take solemn vows without its permission. (Allocution Nunquam fore, 15th December, 1856.)

LIII. The laws for the protection of religious establishments, and securing their rights and duties, ought to be abolished : nay, more, the civil government may lend its assistance to all who desire to quit the religious life they have undertaken, and break their vows. The government may also suppress Religious Orders, Collegiate Churches, and simple Benefices, even those belonging to private patronage, and submit their goods and revenues to the administration and disposal of the civil power. (Allocution Acerbissimum, 27th September, 1852. Allocution, Probe memineritis, 22d January, 1855. Allocution, Cum sæpe, 16th July, 1855.)

LIV. Kings and princes are not only exempt from the jurisdiction of the Church, but are superior to the Church, in litigated questions of jurisdiction. (Letter Apost. Multiplices inter, 10th June, 1851.)

LV. The Church ought to be separated from the State, and the State from the Church. (Allocution Acerbissimum, 27th September, 1852.)

SECTION VII. — ERRORS CONCERNING NATURAL AND CHRISTIAN ETHICS.

LVI. Moral laws do not stand in need of the divine sanction, and there is no necessity that human laws should be conformable to the law of nature, and receive their sanction from God. (Allocution Maxima quidem, 9th June, 1862.)

LVII. Knowledge of philosophical things and morals, and also civil laws may and must be independent of divine and ecclesiastical authority. (Allocution Maxima quidem, 9th June, 1862.)

LVIII. No other forces are to be recognized than those which reside in matter, and all moral teaching and moral excellence ought to be made to consist in the accumulation and increase of riches by every possible means, and in the enjoyment of pleasure. (Allocution Maxima quidem, 9th June, 1862. Encyclical Quanto conficiamur, 10th August, 1863.)

LIX. Right consists. — the material fact, and all human duties are but vain words, and all human acts have the force of right. (Allocution Maxima quidem, 9th June, 1862.)

LX. Authority is nothing else, but the result of numerical superiority and material force (Allocution Maxima quidem, 9th June 1862.)

LXI. An unjust act, being successful, inflicts no injury upon the sanctity of right. (Allocution Ja.idudum ceroimus, 18th March, 1861.)

LXII. The principle of non-intervention, as it is called, ought to be proclaimed and adhered to. (Allocution ..s at ante, 28th September, 1860.)

LXIII. It is allowable to refuse obedience to legitimate Princes; nay more, to rise in insurrection against them. (Encyclical Qui pluribus, 9th November, 1846. Allocution Quisque vestrum, 4th October, 1847. Encyclical Noscitis et nobiscum, 8th December, 1849. Letter Apostolicæ Cum Catholica, 26th March, 1860.

LXIV. The violation of a solemn oath, even every wicked and flagitious action repugnant to the eternal law, is not only not blameable, but quite lawful, and worthy of the highest praise, when done for the love of country. (Allocution Quibus quantisque, 20th April, 1849.)

SECTION VIII.—ERRORS CONCERNING CHRISTIAN MARRIAGE.

LXV. It cannot be by any means tolerated, to maintain that Christ has raised marriage to the dignity of a sacrament. (Apostolical Letter Ad. Apostolicæ, 22nd August, 1851.)

LXVI. The sacrament of marriage is only an adjunct of the contract, and separable from it, and the sacrament itself consists in the nuptial benediction alone. (Id. ibid.)

LXVII. By the law of nature, the marriage tie is not indissoluble, and in many cases divorce, properly so called, may be pronounced by the civil authority. (Id. ibid.; Allocution Acerbissimum, 27th September, 1852.)

LXVIII. The Church has not the power of laying down what are diriment impediments to marriage. The civil authority does possess such a power, and can do away with existing impediments to marriage. (Let. Apost. Multiplices inter, 10th June, 1851.)

LXIX. The Church only commenced in later ages to bring in diriment impediments, and then availing herself of a right not her own, but borrowed from the civil power. (Let. Apost. Ad. Apostolicæ, 22d August, 1851.)

LXX. The canons of the Council of Trent, which pronounce censure of anathema against those who deny to the Church the right of laying down what are diriment impediments, either are not dogmatic, or must be understood as referring only to such borrowed power. (Let. Apost. ibid.)

LXXI. The form of solemnizing marriage prescribed by the said Council, under penalty of nullity, does not bind in cases where the civil law has appointed another form, and where it decrees that this new form shall effectuate a valid marriage. (Id. ibid.)

LXXII. Boniface VIII. is the first who declared, that the vow of chastity pronounced at Ordination annuls nuptials. (Id. ibid.)

LXXIII. A merely civil contract may, among Christians, constitute a true marriage, and it is false, either that the marriage contract between Christians is always a sacrament, or that the contract is null if the sacrament be excluded. (Id. ibid., Letter to King of Sardinia, 9th September, 1852. Allocution Acerbissimum, 27th September, 1852; Multis gravibusque, 17th December, 1860.)

LXXIV. Matrimonial causes and espousals belong by their very nature to civil jurisdiction. (Let. Apost., 22d August, 1851. Allocution Acerbissimum, 27th September, 1859.)

N.B.—Two other errors may tend in this direction, those upon the abolition of the celibacy of Priests, and the preference due to the state of marriage over that of virginity. These have been proscribed; the first in the Encyclical " Qui pluribus," November 9, 1846; the second in the Letters Apostolical " Multiplices inter," June 10, 1851.

Section IX.—Errors Regarding the Civil Power of the Sovereign Pontiff.

LXXV. The children of the Christian and Catholic Church are not agreed upon the compatibility of the temporal with the spiritual power. (Let. Apost. Ad. Apostolicæ, 22d August, 1851.)

44

LXXVI. The abolition of the temporal power, of which the Apostolical See is possessed, would contribute in the greatest degree to the liberty and prosperity of the Church. (Al. Quibus quantisque, 20th April, 1849.)

N. B.—Besides these errors, explicitly noted, many others are impliedly rebuked by the proposed and asserted doctrine, which all Catholics are bound most firmly to hold, touching the temporal Sovereignty of the Roman Pontiff. These doctrines are clearly stated in the Allocutions "Quibus quantisque," April 20, 1859, and " *Si semper antea*," May 20, 1850; Letters Apost. " *Quum Catholica Ecclesia*," March 26, 1860 ; Allocutions " *Novas*," September 28, 1860 ; "*Jamdudum*," March 18, 1861, and " *Maxima quidem*," June 9, 1862.

SECTION X.—ERRORS HAVING REFERENCE TO MODERN LIBERALISM.

LXXVII. In the present day, it is no longer expedient that the Catholic Religion shall be held as the only Religion of the state, to the exclusion of all other modes of Worship. (Allocution Nemo vestrum, 26th July, 1855.)

LXXVIII. Whence it has been wisely provided by law, in some countries called Catholic, that persons coming to reside therein shall enjoy the public exercise of their own worship. (Allocution Accsbissimum, 27th September, 1852.)

LXXIX. Moreover it is false, that the civil liberty of every mode of worship, and the full power given to all of overtly and publicly manifesting their opinions and their ideas, of all kinds whatsoever, conduce more easily to corrupt the morals and minds of the people, and to the propagation of the pest of indifferentism. (Allocution Nunquam fore, 15th December, 1856.)

LXXX. The Roman Pontiff can, and ought, to reconcile himself to, and agree with progress, liberalism, and civilization as lately introduced. (Allocution Jamdudum cernimus, 18th March, 1861.)

PRINTED BY J. G. MOYLAN, "CANADIAN FREEMAN" OFFICE, 74 CHURCH ST., TORONTO.

www.ingramcontent.com/pod-product-compliance
Lightning Source LLC
Chambersburg PA
CBHW021439090426
42739CB00009B/1560